English for
Sustainable Development

英語でSDGsを実践する

山本有香　新多了

KENKYUSHA

https://www.un.org/sustainabledevelopment/

はじめに

　20世紀に主流であった知識・スキル伝達型の「伝統的教育観」（traditional pedagogy）に対して、21世紀は「変容的教育観」（transformative pedagogy）の時代と呼ばれます[1]。「変容」の対象は、「自己」と「社会」です。

　「自己変容（変革）」とは、自分のアイデンティティを自ら構築することを意味します。変化の激しい現代のグローバル社会では、次々に新しいツールや考えが登場しています。このような時代には、「主体的に学ぶ力」、つまり、自ら課題を設定し、行動（解決）し、ふり返り、次のアクションにつなげていく力が求められます。この学びのサイクルをくり返すことで、どんな環境にも適応し成長を続ける「生き抜く力」を身につけることができるようになります。

　もう一つの「社会変容（変革）」には、地域社会や国内外の様々な問題に関心を持ち、自分の生きる世界をより良い場所へ変えていこうとする姿勢が求められます。社会には常に数多くの問題が存在しますが、それらを地道に解決することで、私たちの住む世界をより良い場所に変えていくことができます。そのような態度を育てることも「変容的教育観」の目的です。

　本書では、英語を使ってSDGs（Sustainable Development Goals）を学ぶことを通して、**変容的教育観の「自己と社会を変革する力」の育成**を目指します。SDGsは2015年9月の国連サミットで採択された、国連加盟193カ国が共有する国際社会の共通目標です。SDGsは17の大きな目標と169のターゲット目標で構成され、2030年までの達成目標期限を定めています。現代のグローバル社会は、環境問題、貧困、差別など様々な問題・課題を抱えています。これは、途上国だけの問題ではなく、日本のような先進国にも起きている問題です。つまり、SDGsは地球市民である私たち全てが当事者として考えるべき課題であり、その達成のためには、異なる文化・価値観を持つ者と交流し、他者の視点に立って考え、共に協力し解決していくことが求められます。

　私たちがSDGsをテーマとした英語教育を通じて最終的に目指すのは、社会的な課題に関心を持ち、深く考えながら他者とともに行動を起こす力の育成です。こうした汎用的能力である「コンピテンス」こそが、複雑で変化の激しい現代のグローバル社会を**「生き抜く力」**だと考えています。本書は、SDGsを通じて、どのような地球規模の課題・目標があるのか、個人レベル・社会レベルでどのような課題解決方法があり、私たちはどう行動すべきなのか、深く考えるための様々なタスク・プロジェクトを提供します。こうした活動に英語を使って取り組むことで、多様な課題に対して語れる内容を持ち、高い思考力を用いて、他者と協働しながら課題解決ができるグローバル人材を育成したいという強い思いから本書を書きあげました。

　この書籍を執筆するにあたり、編集者の方々を始め、学生の皆さんに心から感謝の意を表します。

1　Cummins, J. (2004). Using information technology to create a zone of proximal development for academic language learning: A critical perspective on trends and possibilities. In C. Davidson (ed.) *Information technology and innovation in language education* (pp. 105-126). Hong Kong: Hong Kong University Press.

本書の枠組み

　本書はCLIL（Content and Language Integrated Learning）を基盤としています。CLILとは、教科内容と言語を同時に学ぶ教育アプローチです。CLILでは「4C」（Content, Communication, Cognition, Culture）を重視します。つまり、私たちが生きる社会と深く関わるContentについて、他者と議論・対話し（Communication）、クリティカルに思考する活動（Cognition）を通じて、他者と社会について理解を深め自分のアイデンティティ（Culture）を創ることを目指します。

　本書の各ユニットは、以下のように4Cを基盤とした枠組みで構成します。

◆ Content（内容）：SDGs（Sustainable Development Goals）で掲げられている17の持続可能な開発目標（貧困、飢餓、健康、教育、ジェンダー、水、エネルギー、仕事と経済成長、産業、平等、持続可能な都市計画、環境、平和、パートナーシップなど）について取り上げます。
◆ Communication（言語）：SDGsに関する理解を通じて高度な言語能力（academic language proficiency）を育成するため、下記のアカデミックスキルの習得を目指します。
　▶ 各分野について理解を深めるために必要な専門的語彙や語彙学習のストラテジーの習得
　▶ 他者と議論するためのディスカッションスキル
　▶ Contentを理解するためのリーディングスキル
　▶ Contentを理解するためのリスニング及びノートテーキングスキル
　▶ Contentを説明するためのプレゼンテーションスキル
◆ Cognition（思考）：特に高度な思考力（Higher Order Thinking Skills [HOTS]）に焦点を置き、深く考える力の育成を促します。講義で学んだ知識やリーディングから得た情報についてアウトラインやサマリーを書くことにより、分析する力や評価する力を身につけます。そして、課題に対する新たな解決策を見つける創造的な活動にも取り組みます。
◆ Culture（アイデンティティ）：ペア・グループワークを通じて、外国文化理解にとどまらず、異なる国・地域はもちろん、他者を深く理解し、共通の課題を解決するために協働する力の育成を目指します。

　本書では、国連の持続可能な開発目標（SDGs）に関連するトピックについて取り上げます。SDGsについての理解を深めながら、学習ストラテジーに関する意識を高め、語彙力の強化を目指します。また、クリティカル・シンキングを使った課題中心のディスカッションに参加し、各講義で理解した内容を分析するための様々なタスクを設計しています。各コンテンツについて理解した後、学習者は関連するトピックについてのプレゼンテーションを行います。

　このCLILの講座を通じて、学習者は下記の点について学びます。
　1）流暢かつ正確に英語を読むためのアカデミック・リーディングスキル（L）
　2）明確に構成された講義を理解し、要点をまとめる方法（L）
　3）各講義の理解に必要な学術用語（L）

4）ディスカッションやプレゼンテーションで、自分の考えを提示したり、質問をしたり、他者の視点や意見をさらに発展させる方法（L）

5）様々なタイプの資料を比較対照する方法（C）

6）対象となる学術分野の知識を使い、ディスカッションやプレゼンテーションを通じて自国と他国の文化とのつながりを築く方法（C）

7）ディスカッションとプレゼンテーションにおいて協力的なチームワークを発揮する方法（C）

＊L＝言語の目標、C＝コンテンツの目標

This textbook adopts the CLIL (Content and Language Integrated Learning) educational approach, wherein subject content and language are taught concurrently. Emphasizing the '4Cs' (Content, Communication, Cognition, and Culture), CLIL seeks to enhance students' understanding of others and society. It aims to foster the development of their own identity (Culture) through discussions and dialogues with others (Communication), as well as engaging in critical thinking activities (Cognition) deeply embedded in the society where we live.

Each chapter is structured around a framework based on the 4Cs as follows:

◆ **Content**: Seventeen Sustainable Development Goals (SDGs) are covered in the text, spanning areas such as poverty, hunger, health, education, gender, water, energy, jobs and economic growth, industry, equality, sustainable urban planning, environment, peace, partnerships, etc.

◆ **Communication**: To enhance academic language proficiency by delving into the SDGs, the textbook aims to foster the following academic skills:

▶ Learning specific terms and vocabulary learning strategies necessary to deepen understanding in each area.

▶ Cultivation of discussion skills for effective engagement with others.

▶ Development of reading skills to comprehend the content.

▶ Acquisition of listening skills and note-taking skills to facilitate content understanding.

▶ Polishing of presentation skills for articulating the content effectively.

◆ **Cognition:** The textbook promotes the cultivation of thinking skills, emphasizing higher-order thinking skills (HOTS). Students refine their capacity to analyze and evaluate knowledge gained through lectures and readings by writing outlines and summaries. Additionally, they participate in creative activities to generate new solutions to problems.

◆ **Culture (Identity):** This extends beyond merely comprehending foreign cultures; it encompasses cultivating a profound understanding of individuals who differ from oneself and fostering the capacity to collaborate in addressing shared challenges. Engaging in pair and group activities, students refine their ability to collaboratively tackle common issues, all the while appreciating and integrating diverse perspectives.

This textbook will cover topics related to the United Nations' Sustainable Development Goals (SDGs). While deepening our understanding of the SDGs, we aim to raise awareness of learning strategies and strengthen vocabulary skills. Additionally, we have designed task-centered discussions using critical thinking, where participants will analyze the content they have learned in each lecture. After comprehending each piece of content, learners will give presentations on related topics.

Throughout this CLIL course, students will learn how to:
1) develop academic reading skills to promote fluency and accuracy in reading (L)
2) understand a structured lecture and take notes on significant points (L)
3) understand the academic vocabulary necessary to understand each lecture (L)
4) present their ideas, pose questions, and further develop other people's views and opinions in discussions and presentations (L)
5) compare and contrast different sources (C)
6) apply knowledge of the target academic field and make connections between their own and other culture through discussions and presentations (C)
7) show cooperative teamwork in discussions and presentations (C)

*L = Language goal, C= Content goal

Table of Contents

English
for
Sustainable
Development

What are Sustainable Development Goals?

Warm-up

Work in pairs or groups to discuss the questions below.

1. What does "SDGs" stand for?

2. How many Sustainable Development Goals are there in total?
   a. seven   b. seventeen   c. seventy

3. What is the target year for achieving the SDGs?
   a. 2030   b. 2040   c. 2050

4. Do you know anything about SDGs? Explain what you know.

Learning Strategies: Note-taking 1 (Overview)

Discussion: Do you take notes while listening to lectures? Why or why not?
Why do you think it is essential to take notes in lectures?

Here are some steps on how to take notes.

Steps for Taking Notes

Step 1 : Record the main ideas, supporting details, and examples.

Write down only the main points and essential information. Avoid writing down every word.

◆ Use symbols (&, =, @) and abbreviations (govt, e.g., i.e.).

> A new survey = # of female managers at Jp co ↑ but still < 10%.
>
> *A new survey has shown that the number of female managers at Japanese companies has increased but it is still less than 10% of the total number.*

◆ If you miss information, write down only the keywords, leave a space, and get the information later.

Step 2 : After the class, review your notes.

> Studies have shown that you forget around **50 %** of what you learned if you don't review it **within 24 hrs**. Try to habitually review your notes as soon as possible after the lecture. Also, studies show you can retain information better when handwriting than typing your notes.

Step 3 : To help with reviewing, write a summary (5-6 sentences) at the end of your notes. Only include the main ideas and some important details.

> **This lecture was about** the benefits and risks of nuclear power plants. The benefits the speaker mentioned were low carbon emissions, high energy output, and increased energy independence. **On the other hand**, there are certain risks, including the potential for nuclear accidents and the challenge of properly storing and disposing of radioactive waste. **The speaker concluded that** it is essential to consider all the factors before deciding.

Key Phrases

This lecture was about ...

Also, ...

Moreover, ...

However, ...

On the other hand, ...

The speaker concluded that ...

In the end ...

Target Vocabulary

Guess the meaning of target vocabulary words from the context and match each word below with the best definition.

Sentence	Word	Definition
1. SDGs are the world's new action plan to **eradicate** poverty and hunger, fight inequality, tackle climate issues, and achieve sustainable development.	eradicate ( )	a. a general rule
2. Three **principles** underlie the Sustainable Development Goals.	principle ( )	b. assure
3. Global challenges such as **tackling** climate change and eliminating poverty require global solutions.	tackle ( )	c. omission
4. **Ensuring** that this planet is preserved for everyone requires many governments and citizens to work together.	ensure ( )	d. solve
5. The key to tackling discrimination and inequality is getting rid of **exclusion**.	exclusion ( )	e. wipe out

Content

Read the text below and answer the critical thinking questions.

The Sustainable Development Goals — Action Towards 2030

The world population is estimated to increase by 2 billion from 7.7 to 9.7 billion in 2050. If we continue our current lifestyle, we will encounter a shortage of food, fresh water, land, energy, and other natural resources. For this reason, the United Nations launched the 2030 Agenda for Sustainable Development, which consists of seventeen goals at the UN Sustainable Development Summit in September 2015. 5 World leaders from 193 countries agreed to attain these goals to **eradicate** poverty and hunger, fight inequality, tackle climate issues, and achieve sustainable development. The summit ended with negotiations between all governments in the UN, and the goals were put into effect in 2016 to attain them by 2030.

Three **principles** underlie the Sustainable Development Goals or SDGs. First, the 10

SDGs should be universal, i.e., applying to all countries, whether developed or developing. Raising people's awareness of the goals and how to address the issues actively is the sole path to attaining these targets. Global challenges such as **tackling** climate change and eliminating poverty require global solutions. These goals cannot be achieved by a single person or country, and require the support and coordination of 15 numerous governments and citizens to **ensure** that this planet is preserved for everyone.

Secondly, the SDGs are holistic and integrate all dimensions of sustainability: economic, social, and environmental development. The economic dimension includes stimulating economic growth, innovating industries and technology, and improving 20 working conditions. The social dimension involves eliminating poverty and hunger, and increasing the number of healthy citizens. Environmental development covers tackling climate change, using renewable energy, and providing clean water and sanitation for all. All of these dimensions should go hand in hand. For instance, they state that countries should build an infrastructure to support economic development 25 and well-being while ensuring equal access. The infrastructure must also be upgraded without harming the environment and adding to carbon dioxide emissions.

Most importantly, the SDGs state that no one should be left behind. Governments have agreed that goals are met only if they are met for everyone. This means that everyone, regardless of race, gender, religion, and status, should have equal access to 30 education, health care, job opportunities, clean water, and sanitation. The key to tackling discrimination and inequality is getting rid of **exclusion**.

Recently, Japan has held a variety of symposiums and exhibitions related to promoting gender equality, aiming toward decarbonized society, and tackling climate change. The events allowed people to think deeply about global issues and envision 35 the future at both the global and local levels. To make the world a better place, everyone should be aware of the current global situation and change how they think and behave. While the goal may appear ambitious, it aligns with the very needs of the world.

Note-taking

Topic:

1. Main Idea 1

      e.g.,

2. Main Idea 2

      e.g.,

3. Main Idea 3

      e.g.,

Critical Thinking

Answer the following questions about the reading and listening text.

1. What are the SDGs?

2. Explain the three underlying principles of the SDGs.

3. Why are the SDGs essential for the world? Which particular goal are you most concerned about and why?

Summarizing

◆ From your memory, what keywords do you remember from the reading?

Keywords:

◆ Using the keywords, summarize today's lecture in your own words within FIVE sentences.

_____

_____

_____

_____

_____

_____

_____

Reflection

Discuss the following topics with your group.

◆ What did you learn in today's class? What did you find attractive in today's class?

◆ How well did you manage the group activity?

◆ Were you able to take notes effectively?

◆ How can you improve it for next time?

Climate Action

Warm-up

Work in pairs or groups to discuss the questions below.

1. Do you think the climate has changed compared to the past?

2. Have you heard of any news events related to climate change? Give specific examples.

3. What can the Japanese government do to tackle climate change?

4. What can we do as individuals to stop global warming?

Learning Strategies: Note-taking 2 (Outlining)

Outlining is a common way of notetaking when you read a book and listen to a lecture. A good outline gives structure to what you learned from a book or class and makes it easier to understand, review and remember. In addition, the act of notetaking keeps you engaged and focused on your reading and listening.

To use outlining, make sections using headings and subheadings. Then record information under each heading by using bullet points or numbers, as shown below:

Main idea
1. Subtopic
   ▶ Supporting facts / examples
      ◆ Details
2. Subtopic
   ▶ Supporting facts / examples
      ◆ Details

Practice

Take note of the content about 'Climate Action' below by using the outlining method.

Topic:

1.

2.

3.

Target Vocabulary

Guess the target vocabulary words from the context and match each word below with the best definition.

Sentence	Word	Definition
1. We have suffered from **heat waves** every summer in recent years.	heat wave (　)	a. impossible to return to a previous condition
2. The effects of global warming have been **accelerating**.	accelerate (　)	b. making you slightly frightened
3. To avoid the **irreversible** effects of global warming, the Paris Agreement was drawn up in 2015.	irreversible (　)	c. force someone to accept something
4. It is necessary to **impose** a carbon tax on private companies to promote renewable energy use.	impose (　)	d. a prolonged period of abnormally hot weather
5. Climate change is a **daunting** issue for everyone.	daunting (　)	e. move more quickly

Content

Read the text below and answer the critical thinking questions.

Climate Action

Climate change, often called the "climate crisis" in recent years, is a significant threat to our lives. One of the most common outcomes is **heat waves**, as record-setting temperatures become a more frequent occurrence across Japan. The main cause of the increasing temperature is the extensive use of fossil fuels and toxic emissions from factories and automobiles. ⁵

The release of harmful gases, including carbon dioxide (CO_2), into the atmosphere at an increasing rate has further promoted the greenhouse effect. These gases trap the sun's heat in the earth's atmosphere, causing the average temperature to rise. The increased temperatures cause abnormal weather, such as floods, typhoons, droughts, and heat waves. ¹⁰

The effects of global warming have been **accelerating**. The earth's average temperature has risen by about 0.6 degrees Celsius over the 20th century. According to a study conducted by the French National Center for Scientific Research, it is estimated that the temperature will rise by about 5.8 degrees Celsius by 2100. This would be devastating to humans, animals, and the environment. To avoid the **irreversible** effects 15 of global warming, the Paris Agreement was drawn up in 2015, which aims to limit the rise in temperature to 2 degrees Celsius and eliminate global greenhouse gas emissions by 2050. Japan is heavily responsible for combating global warming by achieving the target because it is the fifth highest CO_2 emitting country—nearly 40% is from power plants, half of which are coal-powered. 20

What action should be taken against the climate crisis? One way is to reduce fossil fuel use and promote environmentally friendly renewable energy sources such as sunlight, wind, and ocean. Because such renewable energy is less cost-effective than fossil fuels, it is necessary to take measures such as **imposing** a carbon tax on private companies and tax reductions and exemptions for using renewable energy. 25

Many actions can be taken at the individual level. For example, we can participate in a "divestment campaign." Divestment, the opposite of investment, means eliminating your money invested in unethical work or projects, such as promoting the use of fossil fuels and contributing to the climate crisis. According to research from an NGO, many commercial banks are still channeling billions of dollars into the coal industry, and 30 Japanese banks were among the top three lenders to the coal industry between 2019 and 2021. Like divestment, we can participate in many activities and campaigns relatively quickly, raising awareness about environmental issues and creating opportunities to address the **daunting** issue of climate change.

Critical Thinking

Answer the following questions about the reading and listening text.

1. What is the main cause of increasing temperature?

2. How does global warming occur?

3. What is the Paris Agreement?

4. What actions can individuals take to combat climate change, in addition to divestment?

Summarizing

◆ From your memory, what keywords do you remember from the reading?

Keywords:

◆ Using the keywords, summarize today's lecture in your own words within FIVE sentences.

_____

_____

_____

_____

_____

_____

_____

_____

_____

_____

_____

Short Presentation

Take turns and give a short presentation to your group members.

Topic: Give two actions you can take to combat climate change.

> Hello, I'm XX. Today, I'd like to talk about climate change.
>
> There are two suggestions that I would like to make.
>
> First, ... Second, ...
>
> Thank you for listening.
>
> Do you have any questions?

Reflection

Discuss the following topics with your group.

◆ What did you learn in today's class? What did you find attractive in today's class?

◆ How well did you manage the group activity?

◆ Were you able to take notes effectively?

◆ How can you improve it for next time?

Writing

Write an essay on the following topic. Make sure you include your introduction, body, and conclusion. Suggested length: 120-150 words.

What are the best ways for individuals and communities to tackle climate change and move towards a more sustainable future?

Clean Energy

Warm-up

Work in pairs or groups to discuss the questions below.

1. What sources do clean energy include? Give examples.

2. What is the primary source of energy in Japan?

3. What sort of clean energy will we use in the future?

Learning Strategies: Reading 1 (Previewing)

What is previewing?

It is a reading strategy that you recall relevant knowledge about the text and set purposes for reading before reading it. By previewing, you are better prepared for reading and are able to understand the text more deeply.

How do you use previewing?

1. Decide the genre of the text—fiction or non-fiction by looking at basic information and the format (e.g., author, title, visuals). Find information about the characters, setting, and plot if the text is fiction. If the text is non-fiction, find the subject, the aims of the text, and the structure.

2. Predict what is written in the text using your knowledge and experiences. It would be helpful to make questions about the text. These predictions and questions motivate

you and keep you focused while reading.

3. (While reading) Write down important points while reading the text.

4. (After reading) Reflect on the text after reading.

Practice

Choose a text that you like to read (e.g. news article, short novel stories). Follow the above previewing steps. After completing all steps, think about how helpful the previewing strategy is. You can make your previewing steps.

Target Vocabulary

Guess the target vocabulary words from the context and match each word below with the best definition.

Sentence	Word	Definition
1. Carbon dioxide gases come directly from burning fossil **fuels**.	fuel ( )	a. an amount of gas, heat, light, etc. that is sent out
2. There are toxic **emissions** from factories.	emission ( )	b. not continuous
3. Shifting to renewable energy sources is **paramount** for making life sustainable.	paramount ( )	c. not expensive
4. Solar and wind energy are **intermittent**.	intermittent ( )	d. more important than anything else
5. Advancing technology makes renewable energy more accessible, **affordable**, and efficient.	affordable ( )	e. a substance that is used to provide heat or power.

Content

Read the text below and answer the critical thinking questions.

Clean Energy

A tremendous amount of carbon dioxide gases is being released into the atmosphere at an increasing rate due to human activity, causing what is known as the greenhouse effect. Carbon dioxide gases come directly from burning fossil **fuels** for electricity generation and toxic **emissions** from factories, automobiles, etc. In addition, fossil fuels, also called exhaustive energy sources, are limited, so fossil fuels—organic 5 remains of prehistoric plants and animals—cannot be used extensively forever. It is estimated that we have consumed about 40% of the world's oil. If we keep using fossil fuels at the present rate, we will run out of oil and gas within 50 years.

Shifting to renewable energy sources would be **paramount** for making life sustainable for the present and future generations. Renewable energy has many 10 benefits. For example, it does not directly cause greenhouse gas emissions and can decrease pollution. Renewable energy is, well, "renewable"; once renewable energy facilities are built, the costs of the energy source—sunlight, wind, and tidal power—would be minimal.

While renewable energy has many advantages, they are only minimally used—just 15 13% of our energy consumption is renewable energy. This is because there are several hurdles to overcome. First, it is difficult for renewable energy sources to generate power on the same large scale as fossil fuels. For example, solar plants must be located in areas with plenty of sunshine year-round, such as deserts. Second, both solar and wind energy are **intermittent**. They only generate power while the sun is shining or 20 while the wind is blowing, so batteries with higher energy density and storage capacity are needed.

Despite these technological challenges, a shift to renewable energy sources would significantly contribute to reducing greenhouse gas emissions and pollution caused by fossil fuels. Many companies are taking the initiative to move away from fossil fuels 25 and promote clean energy. For example, a major Japanese railway company switched to power generated only by renewable energy sources—solar power, wind power, hydropower, and geothermal power—in 2022. In doing so, the company has achieved zero carbon dioxide emissions for all its train networks and stations, including vending machines, security cameras, and lighting. Advancing technology makes renewable 30 energy more accessible, **affordable**, and efficient. Many more companies need to take on the challenge of combating climate change.

Critical Thinking

Answer the following questions about the reading and listening text.

1. What are fossil fuels made of?

2. Why is shifting to renewable energy sources important?

3. Why is use of renewable energy still limited?

4. Do you know any companies contributing to reducing greenhouse gas emissions and pollution? What actions do these companies take?

Summarizing

◆ From your memory, what keywords do you remember from the reading?

Keywords:

◆ Using the keywords, summarize today's lecture in your own words within FIVE sentences.

_____

_____

_____

_____

_____

_____

_____

_____

Short Presentation

Take turns and give a short presentation to your group members.

Topic: Give two examples of companies and or organizations to promote renewable energy use.

> Hello, I'm XX. Today, I'd like to talk about renewable energy.
>
> There are two examples of using renewable energy.
>
> First, ... Second, ...
>
> Thank you for listening.
>
> Do you have any questions?

Reflection

Discuss the following topics with your group.

- ◆ What did you learn in today's class? What did you find attractive in today's class?

- ◆ How well did you manage the group activity?

- ◆ Were you able to take notes effectively?

- ◆ How can you improve it for next time?

Writing

Write an essay on the following topic. Make sure you include your introduction, body, and conclusion. Suggested length: 120-150 words.

Do you think that the government should promote nuclear power to ensure sufficient electricity?

Clean Water and Sanitation

Warm-up

Work in pairs or groups to discuss the questions below.

1. What roles does clean water play besides drinking?

2. What problems do you think developing countries have with water? Can you guess how they collect water?

3. How can we solve the water shortage problem?

Learning Strategies: Discussion 1 (Expressing opinions)

It is essential to ask and give opinions to develop ideas in discussion. Asking for opinions helps you to know about other people's ideas and to activate the discussion. To ask and give opinions, use the phrases:

Asking for opinions

What do you think about …

What's your opinion?

Giving opinions

In my opinion, …

I think/believe/suppose that …

I would argue that …

Practice

Discuss the following topics. Use the phrases to ask and give opinions.

- Should students study abroad?
- Should students do a part-time job?
- Should students live alone or with their families?

Target Vocabulary

Guess the target vocabulary words from the context and match each word below with the best definition.

Sentence	Word	Definition
1. Water **scarcity** is common, especially in developing countries.	scarcity ( )	a. offering a choice between two or more things
2. Access to clean water helps us avoid various **infectious** diseases.	infectious ( )	b. a situation in which something is not easy to get
3. He designed a tool to provide an **alternative** water source.	alternative ( )	c. start using a plan or system
4. A company has challenged the issue by providing a **portable** toilet.	portable ( )	d. light and small enough to be easily carried
5. The company has **implemented** its portable toilets in many countries.	implement ( )	e. able to be passed from one person, animal or plant to another

Content

Read the text below and answer the critical thinking questions.

Clean Water and Sanitation

If you were to view the earth from space, you might be surprised by how much of our planet is covered by the ocean. This image of a "water planet" gives us the impression that we are surrounded by abundant water. However, the amount of usable fresh water is surprisingly small. It is estimated that fresh water only makes up three percent of all the water on Earth. Furthermore, most of the fresh water is not readily ⁵ accessible because it is in frozen glaciers—only 0.8 percent is available for use. Thus, water **scarcity** is a widespread problem in many parts of the world, especially in developing countries.

Access to clean water is indispensable for everyone—it plays a vital part in the nutrition of individual health. Contaminated water can lead to various illnesses, such as diarrhea and **infectious** diseases. Despite its necessity, the human right to water was not recognized until recent years. In the aftermath of the Second World War, the Universal Declaration of Human Rights was issued in 1948, stipulating that we are all entitled to freedom from slavery and discrimination. However, it did not state free access to water because it was considered obvious then. In 2010, the UN officially recognized and declared access to safe and clean drinking water and sanitation as a human right, implying that we are in a state of shortage of clean water.

There have been many attempts at resolving the problem of water scarcity. An Italian architect, Arturo Vittori, designed the Warka Water Tower to provide an **alternative** water source for rural areas where people must walk miles every day to carry water from rivers to their homes. The tower is made from bamboo trees which collect moisture from the air—through rain, fog, and dew—and water is brought down through natural processes such as gravity, condensation, and evaporation. This structure enables people to receive approximately 100 liters of water a day.

According to a study conducted in 2017, as many as 820 million people do not have access to a basic toilet facility and are forced to relieve themselves in open areas. A Japanese organization has collaborated with a company to develop a **portable** toilet. The portable toilet made by a Japanese company can be easily installed and rinsed with only 200 ml of water. The company launched the "Toilets for All" initiative and has **implemented** its portable toilets in many countries across Asia and Africa.

Critical Thinking

Answer the following questions about the reading and listening text.

1. What percentage of the earth's water can be used?

2. Why was the importance of water not mentioned in the Universal Declaration of Human Rights?

3. How does Warka Water Tower collect water?

4. What can we do to solve the water shortage problem?

Summarizing

◆ From your memory, what keywords do you remember from the reading?

    Keywords:

◆ Using the keywords, summarize today's lecture in your own words within FIVE sentences.

_____

_____

_____

_____

_____

_____

_____

_____

_____

_____

Short Presentation

Take turns and give a short presentation to your group members.

Topic: Give two actions you can take to solve the water shortage problem.

> Hello, I'm XX. Today, I'd like to talk about how we can solve the water shortage problem.
>
> There are two suggestions that I would like to make.
>
> First, . . . Second, . . .
>
> Thank you for listening.
>
> Do you have any questions?

Reflection

Discuss the following topics with your group.

◆ What did you learn in today's class? What did you find attractive in today's class?

◆ How well did you manage the group activity?

◆ Were you able to take notes effectively?

◆ How can you improve it for next time?

Writing

Write an essay on the following topic. Make sure you include your introduction, body, and conclusion. Suggested length: 120-150 words.

What actions can developed countries take to overcome worldwide water scarcity?

Life below Water

Warm-up

Work in pairs or groups to discuss the questions below.

1. Have you ever been to the sea and felt dirty?

2. Have you heard the term, "overfishing"? What do you think overfishing means?

3. What actions should the government take to protect the marine environment?

4. What actions can individuals take to protect the marine environment?

Learning Strategies: Note-taking 3 (Using Symbols)

If you want to take notes quickly and efficiently, you should use notetaking symbols. These will help you record the necessary information while listening to a lecture in class.

Look at the following symbols, which are familiar to most people. Guess and write down the meaning for each.

Example: ↑ (increase)

↓	→	=	<	>
@	?	/	&	#
×	$	∴	≠	

Target Vocabulary

Guess the target vocabulary words from the context and match each word below with the best definition.

Sentence	Word	Definition
1. We have seen a **proliferation** of plastic waste.	proliferation ( )	a. prevent someone from doing something easily
2. We should reduce our dependency on **disposable** items.	disposable ( )	b. make something less harmful
3. Many organizations are trying to **mitigate** the plastic waste problem.	mitigate ( )	c. the fact of something increasing a lot
4. Their efforts are **hampered** by the financial cost.	hamper ( )	d. intended to be thrown away after use
5. You can choose seafood with a **distinctive** blue label.	distinctive ( )	e. marking something as clearly different from others

Content

Read the text below and answer the critical thinking questions.

Marine Resources Protection

As far as we know, Earth is the only planet in our solar system where life exists. The earliest known life forms emerged in the sea 3.5 billion years ago and moved onto land 400 million years ago, evolving into plants, insects, amphibians, and other life forms. All living creatures, including humans, depend on bodies of water for food, energy, and hydration. 5

Despite the necessity of water, we have severely damaged the bodies of water and other precious marine resources. Many marine animals are dying from plastic garbage in the world's oceans. Japan is one of the world's biggest plastic waste producers— second only to the United States—and this trend has accelerated in recent years. We have seen a **proliferation** of plastic waste such as water bottles, polystyrene netting, 10 and **disposable** food containers. To make matters worse, only nine percent of plastic is recycled worldwide; the rest is incinerated, sent to landfills, or lost to waterways and oceans.

Because plastics require hundreds of years or more to degrade, plastic waste has accumulated in the ocean, polluting the waters and killing marine animals. The World 15 Wildlife Fund (WWF) estimates that ocean plastic pollution will quadruple by 2050. There are many organizations like WWF trying to **mitigate** the problem, but they are **hampered** by the financial cost. Thus, governments and manufacturers must provide financial incentives to reduce plastic waste. Consumers like us also need to contribute to tackling this daunting issue by shrugging off our dependency on single-use 20 products—items that are used only once and then disposed of. Refusing single-use products such as plastic straws and bags is an important step toward solving the problem.

Overfishing is another issue threatening the marine environment due to technological advancements that have made fishing in excessively large quantities 25 possible. Overfishing disturbs the ocean ecosystems and the billions of people who rely on seafood as a major source of protein; without sustainable management, our fisheries will collapse, leading to a food crisis.

To encourage sustainable fishing, an international NGO, the Marine Stewardship Council (MSC), uses a blue "eco-label" to identify seafood that has come from 30 sustainable fisheries certified to its standards. This MSC label has been displayed on tens of thousands of products in over one hundred countries around the world. If you want to contribute to maintaining and improving the ocean's health, you can choose seafood with the **distinctive** blue label. Our understanding and actions play a vital role in protecting the ocean resources and our livelihoods for the future.   35

Critical Thinking

Answer the following questions about the reading and listening text.

1. How long had creatures spent in the sea until moving onto the land?

2. What is the situation with plastic waste in Japan?

3. What is needed to solve the plastic waste problem?

4. How can we solve the overfishing problem?

Summarizing

◆ From your memory, what keywords do you remember from the reading?

    Keywords:

◆ Using the keywords, summarize today's lecture in your own words within FIVE sentences.

_____

_____

_____

_____

_____

_____

_____

Short Presentation

Take turns and give a short presentation to your group members.

Topic: Give two actions to solve the ocean pollution problem.

> Hello, I'm XX. Today, I'd like to talk about ocean pollution.
>
> There are two actions to solve the ocean pollution problem.
>
> First, ... Second, ...
>
> Thank you for listening.
>
> Do you have any questions?

Reflection

Discuss the following topics with your group.

◆ What did you learn in today's class? What did you find attractive in today's class?

◆ How well did you manage the group activity?

◆ Were you able to take notes effectively?

◆ How can you improve it for next time?

Writing

Write an essay on the following topic. Make sure you include your introduction, body, and conclusion. Suggested length: 120-150 words.

What new technology can you think of to reduce plastic wastes?

Life on Land

Warm-up

Work in pairs or groups to discuss the questions below.

1. Have you heard of any news events related to biodiversity and/or deforestation? Give specific examples.

2. Why is cutting down trees (deforestation) bad for animals and plants on land?

3. What should the government do to maintain biodiversity?

4. What are some things we can do every day to help protect the animals that live on land?

Learning Strategies: Discussion 2 (Giving Reasons and Examples)

Supporting your opinions is crucial. This can be done by giving examples and reasons. To ask for and give reasons and examples, use the following phrases.

Asking for reasons/examples	Giving examples
Why do you think so?	For example/instance, …
Can you tell me why?	… such as …
Can you give me an example?	The first example is that …
	To give one example, …
Giving reasons	
Because/As …	
The first reason is that …	
That's why …	

Practice

Discuss the following topics. Use the phrases to ask for and give reasons/examples.

- Should students at primary school go to a cram school?
- Which do you prefer to live in—in a big city or in the countryside?
- Should every student study traditional literature?

Target Vocabulary

Guess the target vocabulary words from the context and match each word below with the best definition.

Sentence	Word	Definition
1. *We should protect species and* ***maintain*** *biodiversity.*	maintain ( )	a. beginning to exist or is happening now
2. *Vegetation* ***regulates*** *temperature.*	regulate ( )	b. the natural environment in which an animal or plant lives
3. *A loss of biodiversity is* ***underway***.	underway ( )	c. reduce in size or importance
4. *Forests provide* ***habitats*** *for various plants and animals.*	habitat ( )	d. control something
5. *Increased deforestation* ***diminishes*** *biodiversity.*	diminish ( )	e. continue to have

Content

Read the text below and answer the critical thinking questions.

Biodiversity and Forest Protection

It is often said that the loss of biodiversity—the variety of plant and animal life in the world—is a severe threat to mankind. Still, it may not be very obvious why we should protect particular species and **maintain** biodiversity. Biodiversity is like a tower of life where all different plants and animals coexist and mutually depend on each other. This biologically diverse system needs to be kept in balance in order to function, ₅ but if blocks are removed one after another, then the tower will become more and more unstable and eventually collapse. A biologically diverse environment provides various important functions; for example, soil purifies water, trees store CO_2, and vegetation **regulates** temperature, all while providing a natural habitat for wildlife species. These functions are no longer available once the ecosystem is lost. ₁₀

Unfortunately, a loss of biodiversity is **underway**. According to a recent report, almost 70% of the world's monitored wildlife was lost between 1970 and 2018. One major cause of biodiversity loss is deforestation—the intentional or accidental removal of trees and other vegetation. Deforestation is occurring on a massive scale, as evident from the destruction of the Amazon rainforests. It is estimated that, at the current rate ₁₅ of destruction, the world's rainforests will completely disappear within 100 years.

Deforestation has devastating impacts on the environment and significantly contributes to climate change—the forestry and agriculture industries are responsible for 24% of greenhouse gas emissions. Because trees absorb greenhouse gases, fewer forests mean more greenhouse gases entering the atmosphere, accelerating the effects ₂₀ of global warming. In addition, forests provide **habitats** for over 80% of plants and animals on land. Thus, increased deforestation destroys these habitats, **diminishing** the biodiversity in rainforests where thousands of species are becoming extinct. However, agricultural activities often promote deforestation. Farmers chop down trees to plant crops or to make room to raise livestock. Countless trees are cut down by logging for ₂₅ wood and paper products. Deforestation is also taking place as a result of growing urbanization.

The effects of deforestation are massive and need to be slowed down or stopped. Various efforts have been made to minimize the impact on our planet—for example, managing forest resources, planting and growing trees (reforestation), and creating new ₃₀ forests (afforestation). Tackling deforestation is particularly crucial in preventing further loss of biodiversity.

Critical Thinking

Answer the following questions about the reading and listening text.

1. Why do we have to maintain biodiversity?

2. What is "deforestation"?

3. What impact does deforestation have?

4. What can we do to maintain biodiversity, in addition to the measures mentioned in the text?

Summarizing

◆ From your memory, what keywords do you remember from the reading?

   Keywords:

◆ Using the keywords, summarize today's lecture in your own words within FIVE sentences.

_____

_____

_____

_____

_____

_____

_____

_____

Short Presentation

Take turns and give a short presentation to your group members.

Topic: Give two actions you can take to protect the forests.

> Hello, I'm XX. Today, I'd like to talk about protecting the forests.
> There are two things we can do to protect the forests.
> First, ... Second, ...
> Thank you for listening.
> Do you have any questions?

Reflection

Discuss the following topics with your group.

◆ What did you learn in today's class? What did you find attractive in today's class?

◆ How well did you manage the group activity?

◆ Were you able to take notes effectively?

◆ How can you improve it for next time?

Writing

Write an essay on the following topic. Make sure you include your introduction, body, and conclusion. Suggested length: 120-150 words.

What actions should the government take to halt the diminishing biodiversity?

Good Health and Well-Being

Warm-up

Work in pairs or groups to discuss the questions below.

1. What health problems does Japanese society have?

2. Have you heard about "well-being"? Do you know anything about it?

3. What mental health problems exist in Japanese society?

4. What should companies do to achieve work-life balance?

Learning Strategies: Reading 2 (Scanning)

What is scanning? It is a reading strategy of searching particular information (e.g., names, numbers, specific facts) in a text. Scanning aims to identify specific words and/or phrases to find an answer or get the main idea.

How do you use scanning?
1. You should have some basic information about the text for effective and efficient scanning. So, it would be effective to do previewing (see Unit 3) before scanning.
2. Decide on a few keywords or phrases you want to know.
3. Look at the text. Don't read the whole text but move your eyes rapidly to locate the

words or phrases.

4. If your eyes catch the key words, then read the sentence including them and the surrounding parts carefully.

How do you use scanning to answer questions in a test?

If you want to use scanning to answer a specific question (e.g., questions in a reading test), the question already gives the keywords.

1. Read the question and find the keywords.
2. Look for the part containing the keywords.
3. When your eyes catch them, read the sentence and the surrounding parts carefully.
4. Read the question again to check whether the part you found is correct.

Practice

Choose a reading text with questions from English tests such as IELTS, TOEFL, TOEIC, and Eiken. Answer the questions **without reading the whole text** by following the scanning steps above.

Target Vocabulary

Guess the target vocabulary words from the context and match each word below with the best definition.

Sentence	Word	Definition
1. *They are closely **correlated** to each other.*	correlate (　)	a. a sign or signal that shows something exists
2. *Good physical and mental health are considered key **indicators** of well-being.*	indicator (　)	b. the number of deaths within a particular society
3. *Newborn deaths **account for** half of the deaths among children under five.*	account for (　)	c. continue to do something even though it is annoying
4. *Maternal **mortality** has fallen by almost 50% since 1990.*	mortality (　)	d. form the total of something
5. *Other serious health problems still **persist**.*	persist (　)	e. be connected and affect each other

Content

Read the text below and answer the critical thinking questions.

Health and Well-Being

It is essential to promote good health and well-being, which are closely **correlated** to each other, for all ages. Well-being refers to the state of being comfortable or happy. Good physical and mental health are considered key **indicators** of well-being. To maintain good health and well-being, we should eliminate many diseases, relieve mental stress, and address various continuous and emerging health issues. 5

Progress has been made in improving health and well-being, such as increasing access to clean water and sanitation, reducing child and maternal mortality, and treating diseases like malaria, tuberculosis, polio, HIV, and AIDS. However, there is still much to accomplish, particularly in developing regions. For example, more than ten percent of children in Africa die before the age of five due to pneumonia, diarrhea, 10 or other diseases. According to UNICEF's report in 2016, 122 out of 1000 children died in Somalia and 120 out of 1000 children died in Nigeria. Child mortality rates of these two countries are extremely high compared to that of Japan, where only two out of 1000 children die by the age of five. In addition, newborn deaths **account for** nearly half of the deaths among children under five worldwide, with 2.6 million 15 stillbirths occurring, and another 2.6 million babies dying in the first 28 days of life every year. Maternal **mortality** has fallen by almost 50% since 1990 but remains very high, about 6%, in developing regions—14 times higher than in developed regions.

Although maternal mortality is no longer a significant issue in developed countries, other serious health problems, particularly mental health issues, still **persist**. Death 20 from overwork, or "karoshi," has been a serious social problem in Japan. Karoshi refers to death caused by brain or heart disease due to work overload or mental disorders triggered by strong psychological strain at work. In the worst cases, overwork and work stress might lead to suicide.

Many companies are working to improve work-life balance in order to reduce 25 overwork, and contribute to a society where people can continue to work in a healthy and fulfilling manner. For example, many Japanese companies have promoted initiatives to create a working environment in which a diverse workforce can maximize employees' abilities through various implementations, such as to reduce working hours by strictly prohibiting overtime work and to support childcare and nursing care. It is 30 hoped that through such attempts in each company, a well-being society can be achieved, in which all people can continue to work in good mental and physical health.

Critical Thinking

Answer the following questions about the reading and listening text.

1. What is "well-being"?

2. What is a severe health problem in African countries?

3. What is a serious health problem in Japan?

4. What measures are Japanese companies taking to achieve work-life balance?

Summarizing

◆ From your memory, what keywords do you remember from the reading?

Keywords:

◆ Using the keywords, summarize today's lecture in your own words within FIVE sentences.

_____

_____

_____

_____

_____

_____

_____

_____

Short Presentation

Take turns and give a short presentation to your group members.

Topic: Give two measures taken by Japanese companies to promote work-life balance.

> Hello, I'm XX. Today, I'd like to talk about promoting work-life balance.
>
> There are two examples of measures to promote work-life balance.
>
> First, . . . Second, . . .
>
> Thank you for listening.
>
> Do you have any questions?

Reflection

Discuss the following topics with your group.

◆ What did you learn in today's class? What did you find attractive in today's class?

◆ How well did you manage the group activity?

◆ Were you able to take notes effectively?

◆ How can you improve it for next time?

Writing

Write an essay on the following topic. Make sure you include your introduction, body, and conclusion. Suggested length: 120-150 words.

What should the government and companies do to achieve work-life balance?

Mid-term project

Warm-up

We have covered the theme of "life and planet" in the first half of the textbook. With your group members, discuss together which following topics you would like to search further. Put a checkmark ☑ and explain your reasons.

- ☐ Climate action
- ☐ Clean energy
- ☐ Clean water and sanitation
- ☐ Life below water
- ☐ Life on land
- ☐ Good health and well-being

To give a successful presentation, make sure your topic is focused. Come up with a good presentation topic with your members.

Presentation Topic:

Researching for Information

1. What do you already know about the issue? Search for further information on the Internet. Report to the other members what you found out.

2. Do you know any companies/organizations tackling the issue? Search for the following information on the Internet.

- ✓ Name of the company/organization:
- ✓ What problem(s) did they find?
- ✓ What are they doing to solve the problem?
- ✓ What actions can you take to tackle the issue?

Sample:

Name of the company: ABC company
Sources: Website (https://www.ABC...)

Problem: Every year, 8 million metric tons of plastic debris is dumped into the ocean.

Solution: 1) Switch to environmentally friendly shopping bags, 2) Eliminate the use of plastic packaging on certain items, 3) Sell eco bags, 4) Charge for shopping bags to promote the use of reusable bags.

My action: Instead of buying coffee in disposable cups from the convenience store, bring my own coffee to school.

Useful Preparation Tips

Here are some tips to make your presentation successful. Creating your PowerPoint Slides with your group members is much faster and more efficient.

Step 1: Create a presentation slide
Open the home screen at Google Slides. This will create and open your new presentation.

Step 2: Share and work with others
Share files with your group members and check whether they can view, edit, or comment on them.

Step 3: Edit and format a presentation
You can add and edit texts and images in your presentation slides.

Presentation Format

Here is a sample presentation format you can follow.

Reasons for choosing the topic	Background of the issue	Actions taken by companies	Actions you can take

1. Reasons for choosing the topic: Why did you decide to work on this topic? How did you react to the issue?

2. Background of the issue: What is the issue?

3. Actions taken by companies: Present several solutions taken by companies/institutions/ organizations.

4. Actions you can take: What actions can you take as a group? How realistic is it?

Useful Expressions

Here are some useful expressions you can use during your group presentation.

<u>**Opening remarks**</u>

Introduce other members
"Good afternoon. My name is Meg and I'd like to introduce the other members of group
1 — Mai, Teru, and Kei.
The title of the presentation is . . . ".

Reasons for choosing the topic
"We decided to search on this topic for two reasons.
First, . . . , Second, . . ."

Tell the organization of your presentation
"Now, Mai will talk about . . . , Next, Teru and Kei will talk about . . . ,
And finally, I will talk about . . ."

Details

Raise the issue

"First, I'd like to talk about the issue of . . .

Recently, . . .

According to . . ."

Actions taken by companies/organizations

"Next, let me introduce some of the actions taken by ABC Company."

Actions you can take

"Finally, we would like to propose two actions we can take to solve the issue. First, . . . ,

Second, . . . "

Closing remarks

"That concludes our presentation. Thank you for listening.

Now, we'd be happy to answer any questions you may have."

Good luck with your presentation!

No Poverty

Warm-up

Work in pairs or groups to discuss the questions below.

1. Can you guess how many people live on less than $1.9 per day?

2. How much money do you spend every day? What do you mostly spend on?

3. What are the causes of poverty?

4. Do you think your home country has a problem with poverty? Give specific examples.

Learning Strategies: Note-taking 4 (Using Abbreviations)

◆ Read the following sentences and see how much information you can understand.

1. # of ppl living on < $ 1.9 /day? > 730 mil ppl

2. Pvty is when ppl can't afford basic thngs e.g., food, water, home / money to buy clothes, ed, + hlth care.

3. There are many causes of pvty, but it can happen when ppl lose their jobs / paid too little.

♦ Look at the following abbreviations and guess their meaning. Write down one possible meaning for each.

govt	dept	yr	hrs	prob
w/	w/o	s/t	K	i.e.
etc	c.f.	e.g.	vs	

Target Vocabulary

Guess the target vocabulary words from context and match each word below with the best definition.

Sentence	Word	Definition
1. Over half of the people living in **extreme** poverty are children.	extreme ( )	a. catch
2. Poverty is when people cannot **afford** basic necessities.	afford ( )	b. farthest
3. Insufficient access to healthcare and **sanitation** can result in serious illnesses.	sanitation ( )	c. manage
4. Escaping poverty can be difficult once someone is **trapped** in it.	trap ( )	d. the practice of keeping the public healthy
5. **Eliminating** poverty is a matter of justice.	eliminate ( )	e. get rid of

Content

Read the text below and answer the critical thinking questions.

Eliminating Poverty

Approximately 730 million people — roughly one in ten people — live on less than $1.90 per day. Over half of those living in "**extreme** or absolute poverty" are children, mostly in sub-Saharan Africa. The cost of just one carton of milk could cover their food, clothes, and shelter. The UN defines extreme poverty as "a condition characterized by severe deprivation of basic human needs, including food, safe   5 drinking water, sanitation facilities, health, shelter, education, and information. It depends not only on income but also on access to services." In simple terms, extreme poverty is when people cannot **afford** necessities such as food, water, shelter, clothing, education and health care.

In Japan, not many people suffer from extreme poverty like starvation. However,   10 there is still a problem with "relative poverty." It is measured by how many households have less than half of the average income. Individuals or families may have enough to meet basic needs, but they still find it challenging to keep up with the average living standards of their society. Relative poverty is often used to understand a country's income inequality and social disparities.   15

Poverty can have multiple root causes, such as climate change, lack of access to basic healthcare and infrastructure, inequality or discrimination, conflict, and instability. Unexpected events like hurricanes, floods, or droughts caused by climate change can push people into poverty by destroying their homes and jobs. Insufficient access to healthcare and **sanitation** can result in serious illnesses which prevent   20 people from succeeding in school or keeping a stable job. Conflict or war may force individuals to leave their homes and possessions behind, leading to impoverishment. Escaping poverty can be difficult once someone is **trapped** in it.

The United Nations plans to end world poverty by 2030. The situation seems complicated, but there are many things we can do to address poverty. For instance,   25 donating clothes, books, medicines, and food to those in need can help to support those in poverty. In addition to donating, you can also volunteer with a charity organization working towards ending poverty. Raising awareness about the problem through a campaign or fundraising can help fight against poverty. Every person has the right to live above the poverty line. **Eliminating** poverty is a matter of justice.   30

Critical Thinking

Answer the following questions about the reading and listening text.

1. What is the difference between extreme poverty and relative poverty?

2. What are the causes of poverty?

3. What are some of the examples given to help eradicate poverty?

4. Can you relate this text to any recent news events?

Summarizing

◆ From your memory, what keywords do you remember from the reading?

Keywords:

◆ Using the keywords, summarize today's lecture in your own words within FIVE sentences.

_____

_____

_____

_____

_____

_____

_____

Short Presentation

Take turns and give a short presentation to your group members.

Topic: Give two actions you can take to solve world poverty.

Hello, I'm XX. Today, I'd like to talk about world poverty.

There are two suggestions that I would like to make.

First, . . . Second, . . .

Thank you for listening.

Do you have any questions?

Reflection

Discuss the following topics with your group.

◆ What did you learn in today's class? What did you find attractive in today's class?

◆ How well did you manage the group activity?

◆ Were you able to take notes effectively?

◆ How can you improve it for next time?

Writing

Write an essay on one of the following topics. Make sure you include your introduction, body, and conclusion. Suggested length: 120-150 words.

Do you think raising Japan's consumption taxes is necessary?

Should the government help homeless people to overcome their poverty?

Zero Hunger

Warm-up

Work in pairs or groups to discuss the questions below.

1. How many people in the world suffer from hunger?

2. What causes world hunger?

3. What should be done to end hunger?

Learning Strategies: Reading 3 (Skimming)

What is skimming? You skim to get the general information about the reading text as quickly as possible.

How do you skim? Jump from keyword to keyword, like throwing the stone in the river. Rather than reading the entire text, focus on the main points.

When it's a long text, carefully read the 1st sentence for each paragraph and the last paragraph. Authors usually summarize the main idea at the end.

Practice Read the following passage and answer the following questions.

The number of people working from home may increase in the future.

Working from home increases productivity and performance. It often results in higher productivity due to . . . People can also save time by not commuting. A study suggests that . . . This will lead to an improved work-life balance.

It can also lead to a healthier life in many ways . . . Working from home makes you more conscious of what you eat. For example, . . . In addition to a healthier diet, you will have more time for physical activities. Overall, . . .

1. What is the passage about?

2. How does the author feel about working from home?

Target Vocabulary

Guess the target vocabulary words from the context and match each word below with the best definition.

Sentence	Word	Definition
1. Although it is a given fact that nutritious food is essential for our health, many people in the world suffer from **hunger**.	hunger ( )	a. give up
2. War has forced them to **abandon** their farms.	abandon ( )	b. having little food to eat
3. It means people do not have equal access to nutritious food that maintains their **immunity** to disease.	immunity ( )	c. not having the right kind of food for good health
4. We need to take action toward eliminating **malnutrition** in the world.	malnutrition ( )	d. protection of the body
5. The goals include zero CO_2 **emissions** from fossil fuel combustion.	emission ( )	e. smoke or gas given off by an engine

Content

Read the text below and answer the critical thinking questions.

Zero Hunger

Although it is a given fact that nutritious food is essential for maintaining our health, many people in the world suffer from **hunger**. It is estimated that one in nine people worldwide does not have enough food. Hunger is one of the leading causes of death in the world. It affects people worldwide, including in developing nations, war zones, and in rich countries with significant economic inequality. 5

Hunger results from various factors, such as climate change, poor infrastructure, poverty, and war and conflicts. Rising temperatures are causing the soil to dry up, making it more difficult to grow food. Also, importing food from other countries can be difficult, especially in places with poor infrastructure. The difficulty of transporting products from one place to another makes them more expensive. Poverty is another 10 cause of hunger. Some people may go hungry because of unemployment, expensive housing, or medical bills. They must rely on government funding, food assistance programs, or donations. Due to war, others may have been forced to leave their homes and **abandon** their farms. Hunger is not only about the price and availability of food. It also means people do not have equal and reliable access to safe and nutritious food 15 such as fresh fruits, vegetables, meat, and dairy products that maintain our health and **immunity** to disease. Poor nutrition affects physical and mental growth, so a healthy diet is vital for well-being. We need to take action toward eliminating **malnutrition** in the world.

In Japan, the term "hunger" doesn't feel like something nearby. Instead, there's a 20 discussion about the problem of food loss, where a significant amount of food is wasted. At the same time, we should not forget that an estimated one in every six or seven children is struggling with poverty. Since 2012, numerous children's cafeterias have been established to offer free or low-priced meals to local children whose families are undergoing financial hardships. 25

Another issue we need to consider is labor shortage scarcity in the agricultural, forestry and fisheries sectors due to the aging population. We might encounter food shortages in the future. To address this issue, Japan's Ministry of Agriculture, Forestry, and Fisheries (MAFF) finalized the green food system strategy on May 12, 2021, which aims to produce and distribute food sustainably to increase the agricultural population 30 and improve the efficiency of agricultural work. The goals include zero CO_2 **emissions** from fossil fuel combustion in agriculture, forestry, and fisheries, a 50% reduction in chemical pesticides, and a 30% reduction in chemical fertilizer. We can end world hunger and related deaths by working together towards the same goal. What action can you take right now? 35

Critical Thinking

Answer the following questions about the reading and listening text.

1. What was the central issue being discussed in this reading?

2. Why do we need a healthy diet?

3. What causes hunger?

4. What actions are taken in Japan to tackle food shortage in the future?

5. Can you relate this text to any recent news events?

Summarizing

◆ From your memory, what keywords do you remember from the reading?

   Keywords:

◆ Using the keywords, summarize today's lecture in your own words within FIVE sentences.

_____

_____

_____

_____

_____

_____

_____

_____

Short Presentation

Take turns and give a short presentation to your group members.

Topic: How can we reduce food loss?

Hello, I'm XX. Do you know . . . ?

Today, I'd like to suggest two ways for reducing food loss.

First, . . . Second, . . .

Thank you for listening. Do you have any questions?

Reflection

Discuss the following topics with your group.

◆ What did you learn in today's class? What did you find attractive in today's class?

◆ How well did you manage the group activity?

◆ Were you able to take notes effectively?

◆ How can you improve it for next time?

Writing

Write an essay on the following topic. Make sure you include your introduction, body, and conclusion. Suggested length: 120-150 words.

How can we grow food more sustainably?

Gender Equality

Warm-up

Work in pairs or groups to discuss the questions below.

1. Do you think we are living in a gender-equal society? Why or why not?

2. What are some of the traditional gender stereotypes in your country?

3. Do you feel traditional gender stereotypes are true? Why or why not?

4. What can we do to eliminate gender inequality?

Learning Strategies: Discussion 3 (Clarifying and Clarification)

When you are a listener, to avoid misunderstanding, it is essential to check whether you understand what the speaker is saying. Try to use the following expressions when you are having a discussion.

> *Sorry, can you repeat that?*   *Excuse me, what did you say?*
> *I didn't catch that.*   *What do you mean?*
> *Can you speak more slowly, please?*   *Could you repeat that, please?*
> *I'm sorry, I don't quite follow you.* *Can you say that again?*

Ensure the listener follows you using the following expressions when you are also the speaker.

> Do you understand?
> Do you know what I mean?
> Do you see what I'm saying?
> Do you follow me?

Target Vocabulary

Guess the target vocabulary words from the context and match each word below with the best definition.

Sentence	Word	Definition
1. This **entails** the concept that they are free to determine their choices without limitations set by stereotypes.	entail ( )	a. a routine task around the house
2. Girls spend time doing their unpaid **chores** at home instead of going to school.	chore ( )	b. act of treating someone badly
3. **Inherited** customs play a big part in how gender roles are assigned.	inherit ( )	c. receive from a person who has died
4. Child marriages may lead to domestic **abuse**, neglect, and complications during childbirth.	abuse ( )	d. spend money or time
5. Countries and organizations should **invest** in girls' education and work towards changing laws and awareness.	invest ( )	e. necessarily involve

Content

Read the text below and answer the critical thinking questions.

Gender Equality

Gender equality should be a fundamental right. Their rights, responsibilities, and opportunities should not depend on their gender. This **entails** that they can develop their skills, think and act for themselves, and determine their choices without limitations set by stereotypes and gender roles. Unfortunately, today, women and girls are denied opportunities because of gender. In certain countries, girls spend time doing ₅ their unpaid **chores** at home instead of going to school. If girls can be educated, become skilled, and have opportunities to get jobs, this will positively impact the world around them, but there are different reasons why this is not the case. For one reason, values, core beliefs, and **inherited** customs play a big part in how gender roles are assigned. This limits how women live their lives. For example, in some countries, ₁₀ women cannot own property or receive an inheritance. In many cultures, child marriage under 18 is still practiced. This may lead to domestic **abuse**, neglect, and complications during childbirth. The primary reasons for mortality in teenage girls stem from these complications. Pregnancy at a young age can impact a girl's health and future, especially if she does not have an education. ₁₅

Even in places where men and women have equal rights legally, there still may be a gender gap in pay, leadership, and representation in government. In Japan, women enjoy equal access to education and healthcare. However, according to the 2023 Global Gender Gap Report from the World Economic Forum (WEF), Japan holds the 125th position out of 146 countries in the overall ranking. Among G7 nations, Japan ₂₀ has the poorest standing. How does the WEF evaluate gender inequality? It examines data on women's status across four key areas: the economy, education, health, and politics. Japan is positioned unfavorably in the politics category due to its low representation of women in parliamentary and ministerial roles. In fact, only 10% of parliamentary lawmakers and 8.3% of ministers are women. Furthermore, Japan has ₂₅ never had a female prime minister. Traditional societal norms make it hard for women to succeed in a political career. People often criticize the government for not doing enough to get women into politics. While others believe that the main problem is that most of the people in charge are men. Additionally, Japan's economic ranking is low. This reflects factors like low female labor force participation and the wage disparity ₃₀ between men and women.

All women and girls should be valued and treated equally as human beings and receive equal opportunities in the social, economic, and political world. For instance, women should have equal opportunities for education and employment, make their own healthcare decisions and become contributing leaders in government. What can we do to eliminate gender inequality? Countries and organizations should **invest** in girls' education and work towards changing laws and awareness so that women can have equal positions and pay. The good news is that the number of women leadership positions worldwide has doubled since the year 2000. The Japanese government aims to achieve a 30% representation of women in executive roles at leading companies by the year 2030. More women are getting the chance to succeed in work and politics; they have more of a voice in making decisions and choices that affect the world.

Critical Thinking

Answer the following questions about the reading and listening text.

1. What was the central issue being discussed in this reading?

2. What is the definition of child marriage? What are some of its risks?

3. How does the WEF evaluate gender inequality? What are some of the reasons contributing to Japan's low ranking?

4. What can we do to eliminate gender inequality?

Summarizing

◆ From your memory, what keywords do you remember from the reading?

Keywords:

◆ Using the keywords, summarize today's lecture in your own words within FIVE sentences.

_____

_____

_____

_____

_____

_____

_____

_____

_____

_____

Short Presentation

Take turns and give a short presentation to your group members.

Topic: Can you relate this text to recent news events?

Hello, I'm XX.

While I was reading this text, it actually reminded me of some news I saw recently.

According to . . . Furthermore, ...

Thank you for listening.

Reflection

Discuss the following topics with your group.

◆ What did you learn in today's class? What did you find attractive in today's class?

◆ How well did you manage the group activity?

◆ Were you able to take notes effectively?

◆ How can you improve it for next time?

Writing

Write an essay on the following topic. Make sure you include your introduction, body, and conclusion. Suggested length: 120-150 words.

Do you think the number of families in which both parents work will continue to increase in Japan?

Should women stay at home to take care of their children?

Quality Education

Warm-up

Work in pairs or groups to discuss the questions below.

1. What does quality education mean to you?

2. How can schools foster a safe and inclusive environment to promote quality education?

3. Do you think you are getting a quality education? Why? Give examples to support your opinion.

Learning Strategies: Note-taking 5 (Noting Numbers and Statistics)

You often hear figures during the lecture; noting them correctly is vital to improving your understanding.

It is easy to follow numbers using commas as your guide. Now try to read out the number.

$$1,234,567,890$$

billion   million   thousand

You can abbreviate and round the numbers using letters when taking notes.

$$24,000 = 24K$$

$$56,000,000 = 56 \text{ mil}$$

$$78,000,000,000 = 78 \text{ bil}$$

Quickly search the Internet and find the figures for the following questions. Make sure you try to use abbreviations and round the numbers when you take notes.

1. How many people live in Tokyo? In Japan?

2. How many students are enrolled in your high school or university?

3. How many people got married last year in Japan?

Target Vocabulary

Guess the target vocabulary words from the context and match each word below with the best definition.

Sentence	Word	Definition
1. *It opens the door to many opportunities to **attain** their dreams.*	attain ( )	a. achieve
2. *If prompt measures are not taken, about 825 million children, which **equates** to half of the global young population, will lack the essential skills.*	equate ( )	b. escape
3. *People living in war zones may be forced to **flee** their countries.*	flee ( )	c. excuse someone from payment
4. *Without **acquiring** a formal education, they have fewer opportunities to earn a sufficient income in the future.*	acquire ( )	d. get
5. *The government is also establishing a system that provides reduced university tuition and **exemptions** for low-income households.*	exempt ( )	e. make or consider to be equal

Content

Read the text below and answer the critical thinking questions.

Quality Education

Through quality education, people can gain the knowledge and skills to stay healthy and learn about global events and their rights. It also helps them get stable jobs, which helps their countries prosper, and opens the door to many opportunities to **attain** their dreams. As people learn more about the world around them, they may care more about global issues. To provide quality education, we need enough teachers, as 5 well as learning resources such as books, computers, supplies, and safe and clean schools. Quality education also means having opportunities beyond basic literacy and numeracy skills. Children who go through a good learning environment become valuable community members. Certain countries, such as Singapore, invest considerable money in education and provide sufficient resources for learning. 10

Although the Sustainable Development Goal aims to ensure that every child receives an education by 2030, approximately 260 million children are still not attending secondary or even primary school. More than half of the children who are not in school live in sub-Saharan Africa. If prompt measures are not taken, about 825 million children, which **equate** to half of the global young population, will lack the 15 essential skills required for future employment within the next ten years.

Instead of going to school, some work to earn money or help care for their families at home. In some countries, girls are prohibited from attending school, or their families do not consider education necessary. Schools are sometimes too far away from home and access to transportation is lacking. Some households may not have enough money 20 to pay for tuition and school supplies. People living in war zones may be forced to **flee** their countries, and their local schools may be destroyed. Even children who make it to school may not get a good education because of overcrowding and a lack of trained teachers. Without **acquiring** a formal education, they have fewer opportunities to earn a sufficient income in the future. People living in poverty are also more likely to get 25 sick, making it harder to keep a steady job.

Countries of the UN are working towards building schools and libraries in developing countries. They also provide teachers with training, supplies, and space to create a better teaching environment. In Japan, the government is trying to tackle the issue by reducing the financial burden of education and making early childhood 30 education more accessible. The government is also establishing a system that provides reduced university tuition and **exemptions** for low-income households.

Quality education can allow people to earn a decent income, and eliminate social class and gender inequality. Learning about other countries and our own can help us create a democratic and peaceful world where everyone is equal.

Critical Thinking

Answer the following questions about the reading and listening text.

1. What was the central issue being discussed in this reading?

2. Why is it important to have quality education?

3. What do we need to provide quality education?

4. What factors inhibit certain children from going to school?

5. To improve the situation, what are certain countries doing?

Summarizing

◆ From your memory, what keywords do you remember from the reading?
Keywords:

◆ Using the keywords, summarize today's lecture in your own words within FIVE sentences.

_____

_____

_____

_____

_____

_____

_____

_____

Short Presentation

Take turns and give a short presentation to your group members.

Topic: Can you relate this text to recent news events?

> Hello, I'm XX. This text reminded me of . . .
>
> Based on XXX news, it was reported that . . .
>
> This is very similar to what I saw on the news recently.
>
> Thank you for listening.

Reflection

Discuss the following topics with your group.

◆ What did you learn in today's class? What did you find attractive in today's class?

◆ How well did you manage the group activity?

◆ Were you able to take notes effectively?

◆ How can you improve it for next time?

Writing

Write an essay on the following topic. Make sure you include your introduction, body, and conclusion. Suggested length: 120-150 words.

◆ Do you think that online courses are as effective as traditional classes?

◆ How can we enhance current standardized tests to more accurately assess the quality of education and student progress?

Decent Work and Economic Growth

Warm-up

Work in pairs or groups to discuss the questions below.

1. What does decent work mean?

2. Does everybody in your home country have decent work?

3. Do you have a part-time job? Is it decent work? Why/why not?

Learning Strategies: Reading 4 (Vocabulary)

To get the meanings of some words, separate their roots from any prefixes or suffixes:

bicycle: bi- / cycle   teacher: teach / -er

prefix   suffix

A prefix is a word part added to the **beginning** of a word to change its meaning or function in a sentence. For example, the prefix re- means "again," so revisit means to visit again.

A suffix is a word part added to the **end** of a word. For example, the suffix -er means "person," so teacher means a person who teaches.

Understanding common prefixes and suffixes can help you figure out unfamiliar English words you encounter. It also improves your spelling skills.

Prefix	Meaning	Examples	Suffix	Meaning	Examples
anti-		antisocial	-able -ible		edible
auto-		autonomous	-an		musician
bene-		benefit	-ant		participant
bio-		biology	-ate		graduate
co-		coauthor	-ee		employee
dis-		disagree	-er		teacher
ex-		ex-wife	-or		conductor
extra-		extraordinary	-ion -tion -sion		information
in-		inability	-ism		capitalism
mal-		malfunction	-ist		scientist
mis-		misunderstand	-ive		massive
mono-		monolingual	-less		useless
multi-		multinational	-logy		anthropology
post-		postwar	-ment		establishment
pre-		prerequisite	-ness		unhappiness
re-		recover	-osis		tuberculosis
sub-		subway	-phobia		claustrophobia
un-		unhappy	-scope		telescope

Target Vocabulary

Guess the target vocabulary words from the context and match each word below with the best definition.

Sentence	Word	Definition
1. When a working environment is comfortable, the community becomes much more **robust**.	robust ( )	a. distributed equally
2. The incident brought increasing attention to the need for companies to **engage** in sustainable management.	engage ( )	b. proper
3. When economic growth is not **inclusive**, more people struggle to find secure and stable employment opportunities.	inclusive ( )	c. strong, healthy
4. As individuals, we can make **decent**, ethical choices when we buy products with the Fairtrade logo showing they were made in ethical working conditions.	decent ( )	d. be worthy or have a right to
5. Workers **deserve** to work in safe, inclusive, and equal conditions.	deserve ( )	e. take part in

Content

Read the text below and answer the critical thinking questions.

Decent Work and Economic Growth

Many people work not only to earn a living but also to feel a sense of purpose. We feel fulfilled when we provide a service to people who need it, or work as a team to achieve a specific goal. Everyone wants to work in a safe and comfortable workplace. When a working environment is comfortable, the community becomes much more **robust**. In a good working environment, employees' health and well-being are 5 protected, and they get paid properly for their work. This can improve their quality of life. In this way, they have more freedom to use their unique skills and provide services, so protecting labor rights and taking appropriate actions against inequalities are essential.

According to the UN, GDP and labor productivity increased globally, but growth 10 has slowed, and inequalities have widened. By 2030, 60% of the world's population will be living in cities, and it is estimated that approximately 470 million workers will be required. In some areas, there are not enough jobs to keep up with the growing number of workers. Therefore, employers do not need to offer ethical, productive work and a fair income for all. Jobs in such places often do not have safe working conditions 15 or social protection for families. A tragic incident occurred in Bangladesh in 2013, where an eight-story garment factory collapsed, killing around 1,500 workers. The incident brought increasing attention to the need for companies to **engage** in sustainable management for ethical, productive, and fair working conditions.

When economic growth is not **inclusive**, more people struggle to find secure and 20 stable employment opportunities. Additionally, some people willing to start or expand their businesses may encounter obstacles as a result of banks denying them loans based on factors such as gender, ethnicity, or disability. These exclusionary actions can lead to stress and tension within the communities. In extreme scenarios, it can even push individuals towards engaging in criminal activities and violence. 25

How can we promote sustained economic growth while creating full and productive employment to reduce poverty and inequality? It is imperative to continually invest in training and education, thereby empowering individuals to transition into secure employment opportunities, irrespective of their socio-economic background or gender. Crowdfunding enables anyone to contribute to starting or 30 growing a business. Technology can also support growing enterprises and job creation.

As individuals, we can make **decent**, ethical choices when we buy products with the Fairtrade logo showing they were made in ethical working conditions. Every worker **deserves** to work in safe, inclusive, and equal conditions. Local communities can ensure inclusive and sustainable economic growth while maintaining workers' work- life balance.   35

Critical Thinking

Answer the following questions about the reading and listening text.

1. What was the central issue being discussed in this reading?

2. What does it mean to have a good working environment?

3. Why is it essential to have a good working environment?

4. What are some reasons people cannot have a decent job?

5. What are some of the solutions provided by the author to promote sustained economic growth?

Summarizing

◆ From your memory, what keywords do you remember from the reading?

Keywords:

◆ Using the keywords, summarize today's lecture in your own words within FIVE sentences.

_____

_____

_____

_____

_____

_____

_____

_____

Short Presentation

Take turns and give a short presentation to your group members.

Topic: Can you relate this text to recent news events?

> Hello, I'm XX. Let me share another case of . . .
>
> According to Professor X, it has been reported that . . .
>
> For example, . . . I believe . . .
>
> Thank you for listening.

Reflection

Discuss the following topics with your group.

◆ What did you learn in today's class? What did you find attractive in today's class?

◆ How well did you manage the group activity?

◆ Were you able to take notes effectively?

◆ How can you improve it for next time?

Writing

Write an essay on one of the following topics. Make sure you include your introduction, body, and conclusion. Suggested length: 120-150 words.

Do you think more employees will work from home in the future?

Do you think work-sharing should be promoted?

Partnerships

Warm-up

Work in pairs or groups to discuss the questions below.

1. What are the most critical SDGs in your country?

2. What does the word "partnership" mean to you?

3. How can we solve global challenges?

Learning Strategies: Discussion 4 (Commenting on an Idea)

It's essential to show that you are listening and understanding what the speaker is saying by giving reactions. While you are having a discussion, try to respond and ask follow-up questions to your group members.

I agree with your point. / I see what you're saying.

I hadn't thought about that. / That's an interesting point.

I see where you're coming from. / That's a valid concern.

I find your perspective intriguing.

You can further expand the discussion by using some follow-up questions.

Can you explain your reasoning a bit more?

Can you share more about how you arrived at that conclusion?

How do you think it applies to what we discussed so far?

Have you considered how it might impact . . . ?

Could you clarify how this aligns with or differs from X's perspective?

What recommendations or actions would you propose based on this insight?

Target Vocabulary

Guess the target vocabulary words from the context and match each word below with the best definition.

Sentence	Word	Definition
1. *We may feel powerless against our **insurmountable** global challenges.*	insurmountable ( )	a. at the very same time
2. *We are all **interconnected**; for instance, the air and water belong to everyone and are never confined to one region.*	interconnect ( )	b. felt or understood in the same way
3. *It would not be **feasible** if only half of the world works toward the goal while the other half pollutes the planet.*	feasible ( )	c. not capable of being conquered or overcome
4. *Collaboration between nations gives us hope to solve global issues requiring equality and **mutual** respect.*	mutual ( )	d. likely to succeed
5. *Every action that we take can tackle multiple issues **simultaneously**.*	simultaneously ( )	e. tie together

Content

Read the text below and answer the critical thinking questions.

Partnerships

We may feel powerless against the **insurmountable** global challenges that we face. It can take work to solve a problem independently. Still, achieving this is attainable when we collaborate through beneficial partnerships at different levels—globally, regionally, nationally, and locally-oriented, including in developed and developing countries. Global challenges that affect us all require global solutions. The SDGs can only be achieved through strong global partnerships and cooperation.

We are all **interconnected**; for instance, the air and water belong to everyone and are never confined to one region. It is everybody's responsibility to make them cleaner, starting with cutting back on CO_2 emissions in the air and reducing plastic waste in the ocean. It would not be **feasible** if only half of the world works toward the goal while the other half pollutes the planet. Problems drift and flow around the world, impacting all of us in one way or another.

Collaboration between nations gives us hope to solve global issues, although this requires equality and **mutual** respect. Groups of people with shared interests need to come together. For example, millions of people are forced to flee their homes due to wars and civil conflicts, persecution, and natural disasters. Protecting the rights of refugees and migrants requires collaboration among countries to provide safe places for them, make sure they get a fair chance for safety, and prevent human trafficking. Solving such large-scale problems is only possible through collaboration.

Fortunately, the pathways toward accomplishing the SDGs are intricately linked and interdependent. Another example is education. Education is a powerful tool to address inequality and the ability to secure decent jobs which also leads to the issue of hunger and poverty. When people have equal opportunities for education, it helps reduce economic and social disparities. Education helps individuals make informed choices and advocate for their rights. When people are educated, they can participate more actively in their communities. Additionally, when more people are educated, it helps the country's economy grow, and that creates more job opportunities and as a result, achieve higher standards of living. Every action that we take can tackle multiple issues **simultaneously**. We are all facing the same problems together, and we are all part of the solution. Who can you partner with in your community to make the world a better place? As Malala Yousafzai said, "We must work . . . not wait. Not just the politicians and the world leaders, we all need to contribute. Me. You. We. It is our duty."

Critical Thinking

Answer the following questions about the reading and listening text.

1. What was the central issue being discussed in this reading?

2. How can we solve global challenges?

3. What is the significance of addressing the issue on a global scale rather than a local one?

4. What are some issues that we need to act on globally?

Summarizing

◆ From your memory, what keywords do you remember from the reading?

Keywords:

◆ Using the keywords, summarize today's lecture in your own words within FIVE sentences.

_____

_____

_____

_____

_____

_____

_____

Short Presentation

Take turns and give a short presentation to your group members.

Topic: Can you relate this text to recent news events?

Hello, I'm XX. While I was reading the text, I was thinking about . . .

Today, many people are suffering from . . . Moreover, . . .

We need to act on this issue globally.

Thank you for listening.

Reflection

Discuss the following topics with your group.

◆ What did you learn in today's class? What did you find attractive in today's class?

◆ How well did you manage the group activity?

◆ Were you able to take notes effectively?

◆ How can you improve it for next time?

Writing

Write an essay on one of the following topics. Make sure you include your introduction, body, and conclusion. Suggested length: 120-150 words.

Which specific SDG challenge do you believe requires collaborative partnerships to address effectively? Why?

How can local communities or schools play a role in forming partnerships to achieve the SDGs?

Final Project

Warm-up

We have covered the theme of "justice and human rights" in the latter half of the textbook. Discuss which topics you would like to search further with your group members. Put a checkmark ☑ and explain your reasons.

- ☐ No poverty
- ☐ Zero hunger
- ☐ Gender equality
- ☐ Quality education
- ☐ Decent work and economic growth
- ☐ Partnerships

To give a successful presentation, make sure your topic is focused. Come up with a good presentation topic with your members.

Presentation Topic:

Researching for Information

1. What do you already know about the issue? Search for further information on the Internet. Report to the other members what you have found out.

2. Do you know any companies/organizations tackling the issue? Search for the following information on the Internet.

- ✓ Name of the company/organization:
- ✓ What problem(s) did they find?
- ✓ What are they doing to solve the problem?
- ✓ What actions can you take to tackle the issue?

Useful Preparation Tips

Here are some tips to make your presentation successful.

Body language

1. Stand straight in a comfortable posture. Avoid crossing your arms.
2. Keep hands by your side. Refrain from touching your hair or placing your hands in your pockets.
3. When you want to emphasize your points, move or lean forward to show that something is essential. Utilizing a pointer or your hand to highlight crucial information is also effective.
4. When you make eye contact, distribute your focus evenly across the entire audience, frequently engaging with each individual rather than focusing on a single point.
5 You should slow your speech by approximately 20% from your usual pace. Focus on clearly enunciating your main concepts and aim to communicate as clearly as possible, using a sufficiently loud voice.

Presentation Format

Here is a sample presentation format you can follow:

| Reasons for choosing the topic | Background of the issue | Actions taken by companies | Actions you can take |

1. Reasons for choosing the topic: Why did you decide to work on this topic? How did you react to the issue?

2. Background of the issue: What is the issue?

3. Actions taken by companies: Present several solutions taken by companies/institutions/organizations.

4. Actions you can take: As a group, what actions can you take? How realistic is it?

Good luck with your presentation!

＜著者紹介＞

山本有香（やまもと・ゆか）
青山学院大学法学部教授。Temple University, Tokyo, Graduate School of Education 英語教授法（TESOL）専攻 修士課程修了。上智大学大学院外国語学研究科（言語学専攻）博士前期・後期課程修了。長年、大学英語授業のカリキュラム開発、教科書執筆や教員養成に携わり、現職。

新多 了（にった・りょう）
立教大学外国語教育研究センター教授。University of Warwick, UK, Centre for Applied Linguistics 修士課程・博士課程修了（PhD in English Language Teaching and Applied Linguistics）。主な著書に、『はじめての第二言語習得論講義──英語学習への複眼的アプローチ』（大修館書店、共著）、『「英語の学び方」入門』（研究社）などがある。

English for Sustainable Development
英語でSDGsを実践する

2023 年 12 月 28 日　初版発行

KENKYUSHA
＜検印省略＞

著　者	山本有香・新多了	
発行者	吉田尚志	
印刷所	図書印刷株式会社	

発行所　　株式会社　研究社

〒 102-8152　東京都千代田区富士見 2-11-3
電話　編集 (03) 3288-7711(代)
　　　営業 (03) 3288-7777(代)
振替　00150-9-26710
https://www.kenkyusha.co.jp/

© Yuka Yamamoto and Ryo Nitta, 2023
Printed in Japan / ISBN 978-4-327-42202-8　C1082
本文デザイン・組版：株式会社 明昌堂
装幀：Malpu Design（宮崎萌美）